CAREER EXPLORATION

Director:
Film, TV, Radio, and Stage

by Lewann Sotnak

Consultant:
Ayesha Adu
Filmmaker

CAPSTONE BOOKS
an imprint of Capstone Press
Mankato, Minnesota

Capstone Books are published by Capstone Press
818 North Willow Street, Mankato, Minnesota 56001
http://www.capstone-press.com

Library of Congress Cataloging-in-Publication Data
Sotnak, Lewann.
  Director: film, TV, radio, and stage/by Lewann Sotnak
  p. cm.—(Career exploration)
  Includes bibliographical references and index.
  Summary: Explains the educational requirements, duties, workplace, salary,
and employment opportunities of the job of director, discussing stage work, movies,
television, and radio.
  ISBN 0-7368-0327-0
  1. Motion pictures—Production and direction—Vocational guidance—Juvenile
literature. [1. Theater—Production and direction—Vocational guidance. 2. Motion
pictures—Production and direction—Vocational guidance. 3. Television—Production
and direction—Vocational guidance. 4. Radio—Production and direction—
Vocational guidance. 5. Occupations. 6. Vocational guidance.] I. Title. II. Series.
PN1995.9.P7 S663 2000
791.43'0233—dc21   99-14631
                                                                          CIP

Editorial Credits
Matt Doeden, editor; Steve Christensen, cover designer; Kia Bielke, illustrator;
  Heidi Schoof, photo researcher

Photo Credits
David F. Clobes, 16, 19, 21 (bottom)
FPG International LLC, 15
Index Stock Imagery, 31; Index Stock Imagery/H.J. Morrill, 11, 38; John
  Coletti, 22; Frank Siteman, 25; Bill Bachman, 28; Kindra Clineff, 40
International Stock/Ryan Williams, cover; Dusty Willison, 6; Jay Thomas, 9;
  Charlie Westerman, 12; Mark Bolster, 33, 35
Photo Network/John Malmin, 42
Unicorn Stock Photos/Joe Sohm, 21 (top); Batt Johnson, 36

Table of Contents

Fast Facts

Career Title	Director
O*NET Number	34056G
DOT Cluster (Dictionary of Occupational Titles)	Professional, technical, and managerial occupations
DOT Number	150.067-101
GOE Number (Guide for Occupational Exploration)	01.03.03
NOC Number (National Occupational Classification-Canada)	5131
Salary Range (U.S. Bureau of Labor Statistics and Human Resources Development Canada, late 1990s figures)	U.S.: $14,000 to $500,000 Canada: $7,000 to $68,500 (Canadian dollars)
Minimum Educational Requirements	U.S.: high school diploma Canada: high school diploma
Certification/Licensing Requirements	U.S.: none Canada: none

Subject Knowledge	Administration; management; fine arts; communications; media; English
Personal Abilities/Skills	Understand the ideas that the author of a script is trying to convey; demonstrate to others how to move or speak to convey these ideas to an audience; speak clearly and loudly; maintain physical and mental energy through lengthy rehearsals and performances
Job Outlook	U.S.: faster than average growth Canada: poor
Personal Interests	Artistic: interest in creative expression of feelings or ideas
Similar Types of Jobs	Managing directors; company managers; booking managers; playwrights; publicity agents; actors; stage managers

Chapter 1

Director

Directors are people who oversee the creation of entertainment productions. These productions include movies, TV shows, music videos, radio programs, and plays. Directors work with writers, performers, and others in the entertainment and news industries to create productions.

What Directors Do

Directors are in charge of a number of tasks. They conduct auditions to find performers. Performers come to auditions to try out for parts in productions. Directors choose the performer who will best act out each part.

Directors conduct auditions to find performers.

Directors help performers understand their parts. Directors might give performers ideas on how to act out their parts. For example, they may help performers discover the best ways to read their lines. They may help performers choose gestures that fit the performers' characters.

Directors work on scripts. Directors help writers create these stories. They help performers understand the scripts. Directors sometimes change scripts during production to make improvements.

Some directors create storyboards for film and TV productions. Storyboards are drawings and diagrams that show the plot of a production. Storyboards help directors divide productions into many scenes. This helps directors plan their production schedules. It also helps them understand how the scenes will fit together.

Directors also supervise production crews. These crews include most of the people on a production set. Production crews may include

Directors help actors choose gestures that fit their characters.

set designers, makeup artists, and camera operators. Directors make sure all the production crew members understand and perform their jobs.

Producers

Directors often work for producers. Producers fund productions. They often choose scripts and hire directors. Producers and directors may work together to select production crews and casts. A cast is a group of performers who work on a certain production.

Directors and producers work together to make other major production decisions. They decide how to film movies and TV shows. They decide whether to film on location or on sets. Productions filmed on location use real buildings and scenery. For example, some directors film movies on location in the mountains. Others may film on sets built to look like mountains.

Directors make sure camera operators and other members of production crews understand their jobs.

Chapter 2

A Day on the Job

Directors' tasks depend on the productions they direct. Stage directors, film directors, TV directors, and radio directors each perform different daily tasks.

Stage Directors

Stage directors are in charge of plays. They supervise the construction of scenery. They work with technicians. These production crew members oversee light, sound, and other items. Stage directors work with costume designers and makeup artists. Together these production crew members make actors look like the characters the actors portray. Directors also set up rehearsal schedules. Rehearsals are practice performances.

Stage directors work with lighting technicians.

Stage directors may begin their days by preparing for auditions, rehearsals, or performances. Stage directors may study scripts or conduct auditions during the early parts of productions. During rehearsals, they may try to identify problems actors are having.

On performance days, stage directors arrive at theaters early. They make sure the sets are ready. They talk with production crews about upcoming performances. Directors supervise actors and other workers as they prepare for performances.

Directors instruct and encourage their casts and crews throughout performances. They do this from back stage. Directors do not appear on stage until a performance is complete. They then may walk onto the stage to bow to the audience.

Film Directors

Film directors are in charge of movies. They spend much of their time planning scenes and deciding how to film them. They plan how

Film directors decide how to film each scene.

each scene will appear on film. They arrange actors and sets. They tell production crew members how to set up lights and sound equipment. They work with camera operators to find the best camera angles.

Directors may choose to film the same scenes many times. Each time they film a

scene is called a "take." Directors often do many takes before they feel a scene is right.

Film directors may spend part of their time working with their producers. They may discuss casts, scripts, or budgets with producers. They also may work with producers and editors to edit films. Directors and producers choose which takes to use when they edit. They also choose which scenes to cut from their films. Directors may spend years on films before the final editing is done.

TV Directors

TV directors often perform many of the same tasks as film directors. But TV directors rarely have as much time to finish their productions. TV stations need directors to finish projects quickly. The stations often show programs each day or week.

Some TV directors are news directors. These directors are in charge of TV news broadcasts. News directors decide how to present the news each day. News directors

TV news directors are in charge of news broadcasts.

supervise reporters, writers, editors, newscasters, and other members of production crews. They choose what news to present first. They decide how much air time to give each story.

Some TV directors work on TV movies and miniseries. These directors must create their productions quickly. They may film fewer takes than film directors do. They also may film more scenes each day.

Radio Directors

Radio directors are in charge of radio programs and schedules. Some radio directors are called program directors. These directors are in charge of scheduling all the programs on a radio station.

Radio directors may be in charge of many different radio programs. Some direct news programs. These directors decide how much air time to give each story. They may help write some of the news broadcasts.

Radio directors set schedules for radio stations.

Other radio directors are in charge of entertainment broadcasts. These include talk shows and music programs. These directors often must find guests for these programs. For example, a radio director may bring in a popular athlete for a sports program.

Some radio directors are in charge of all of a radio station's programs. These program directors decide when to air different programs throughout the day.

Radio directors may spend some days holding auditions for radio announcers. They listen for strong, clear voices. They also try to match voices to situations. For example, a director may hire an announcer with an energetic voice for a morning program. The director may hire an announcer with a soft, soothing voice for an evening program.

Stage Directors

These directors are in charge of live performances. They need basic knowledge of literature, acting, and theater productions. Most stage directors have a high school diploma and four to 10 years of on-the-job training.

Film Directors

These directors are in charge of movies. They need excellent leadership skills to supervise large casts and production crews. Most film directors have a high school diploma and four to 10 years of on-the-job training.

TV Directors

These directors are in charge of a variety of TV programs. They must be fast and efficient to meet deadlines. Most TV directors have a high school diploma. A bachelor's degree and on-the-job training are helpful.

Radio Directors

These directors schedule and direct radio programs. They need organizational skills to fill and balance schedules. Most radio directors have a high school diploma. A bachelor's degree and on-the-job experience are helpful.

Chapter 3

The Right Candidate

Directors need both social and technical skills. They must be good leaders. They need to enjoy working with people. They must communicate well. Directors must be able to work with and understand different personalities. They also need to know how to work equipment such as cameras and lights.

Skills and Interests

Good directors work well with people. They work well in teams. They listen to others' ideas. They communicate their own ideas clearly. They use the talents of all the people working on a production.

Directors need strong reading and writing skills. They must be able to understand scripts

Directors must work well in teams.

clearly. They sometimes have to rewrite parts of scripts during production.

Directors must understand the technical skills involved in a production. Stage, film, and TV directors should understand how to use lighting well. Film and TV directors should know which camera angles work best in different situations. They should know how costumes and makeup work to make characters seem real. Radio directors must understand sound. They must know how audiences react to different voices and sound effects.

Teaching skills also can be important to directors. Directors may help performers understand scripts. They may explain to performers why certain scenes are important. Directors help performers find the best ways to play their characters.

Handling Budgets

Many directors manage budgets. They keep track of how much money is spent during a production. They may have to find ways to

Teaching skills can be important to directors.

keep costs low. They may do this by hiring performers who will work for a certain amount of money. Film and TV directors usually film on sets instead of on location. Directors find the best ways to spend the money they have available.

Directors who handle budgets need good mathematical and organizational skills. They

Skills

Workplace Skills   Yes / No

Resources:
- Assign use of time . . . . ✓ ▯
- Assign use of money . . . . ✓ ▯
- Assign use of material and facility resources . . . . . ✓ ▯
- Assign use of human resources . . . . ✓ ▯

Interpersonal Skills:
- Take part as a member of a team . . . . ✓ ▯
- Teach others . . . . ✓ ▯
- Serve clients/customers . . . . ▯ ✓
- Show leadership . . . . ✓ ▯
- Work with others to arrive at a decision . . . . . . ✓ ▯
- Work with a variety of people . . . . ✓ ▯

Information:
- Acquire and judge information . . . . ✓ ▯
- Understand and follow legal requirements . . . . . ✓ ▯
- Organize and maintain information . . . . ✓ ▯
- Understand and communicate information . . . . . ✓ ▯
- Use computers to process information . . . . . . ▯ ✓

Systems:
- Identify, understand, and work with systems . . . . . ▯ ✓
- Understand environmental, social, political, economic,
     or business systems . . . . ▯ ✓
- Oversee and correct system performance . . . . . ▯ ✓
- Improve and create systems . . . . ▯ ✓

Technology:
- Select technology . . . . ✓ ▯
- Apply technology to task . . . . ✓ ▯
- Maintain and troubleshoot technology . . . . . . ✓ ▯

Foundation Skills

Basic Skills:
- Read . . . . ✓ ▯
- Write . . . . ✓ ▯
- Do arithmetic and math . . . . ✓ ▯
- Speak and listen . . . . ✓ ▯

Thinking Skills:
- Learn . . . . ✓ ▯
- Reason . . . . ✓ ▯
- Think creatively . . . . ✓ ▯
- Make decisions . . . . ✓ ▯
- Solve problems . . . . ✓ ▯

Personal Qualities:
- Take individual responsibility . . . . ✓ ▯
- Have self-esteem and self-management . . . . . . ✓ ▯
- Be sociable . . . . ✓ ▯
- Be fair, honest, and sincere . . . . ✓ ▯

have to keep records about the money they spend. Directors sometimes must keep this information for producers. Producers may refuse to hire directors who handle budgets poorly.

Other Qualities

Directors must be confident. Performers and production crew members expect strong leadership from directors. Directors should be able to make quick decisions. They must be in control of their productions at all times.

Directors must handle unexpected situations with confidence and clear thinking. For example, a performer may suddenly become ill. A director must quickly find a solution to continue the performance schedule. This earns the director the respect of producers and other workers on a production set. It also helps the director meet budgets and deadlines.

Chapter 4

Preparing for the Career

Directors do not always need college degrees to do their jobs. But most successful directors receive education beyond high school. They may study subjects such as drama, English, and communications at colleges and universities.

Education

Students who wish to become directors should earn a high school diploma. High school students should take classes in literature, speech, drama, and writing. These classes help students gain communication skills. Students also should take mathematics and

Students can gain experience as directors by taking part in high school and college film productions.

economics classes. These classes help students learn to handle budgets.

Students can take part in drama clubs and plays. They can try out for parts in school and community productions. They also can volunteer to work with sets, lights, and sound systems for these productions. Students who perform different stage jobs learn a variety of skills that directors need. They also will better understand the people they supervise.

Some directors earn degrees from colleges or universities. These degrees can be in areas such as English, communications, theater, or literature. Some colleges and universities also offer classes in directing.

Other directors attend film schools. These technical schools teach students about all areas of filmmaking. Students learn to direct, operate cameras, write scripts, and perform other filmmaking tasks.

Most radio and TV stations require program directors to have bachelor's degrees. Most

Students can gain skills at colleges, universities, and film schools.

program directors have degrees in communications or business management. Radio and television directors must learn about Federal Communications Commission (FCC) laws. These laws govern the programs radio and TV stations can broadcast.

Gaining Experience

Directors rely on their knowledge and skills to get jobs. But they also need experience. People gain experience in several ways.

Some people gain experience by working as co-directors or production assistants. They help directors with a variety of tasks. They may help to set schedules or work with production crews. This is a good way for young directors to gain skills and experience.

Large productions often require specialty directors for jobs such as music and set design. Directors can gain experience in a variety of tasks by taking these jobs. Producers might notice specialty directors who do good work. Producers may recommend these directors for other jobs.

Some people gain experience by working on small productions. They may act, operate lights, or build sets. People may obtain jobs with more responsibilities as they gain experience.

Directors with a wide range of skills have the best chances of finding jobs.

Some directors start their careers by directing community plays. These directors often work with amateur actors. These actors do not act for a living. Directors can gain experience in teaching, communicating, and other areas by directing these productions.

Other directors gain experience by writing and producing their own films. These directors may write scripts, find actors, and operate cameras. They may edit their material after they finish filming. They can gain a wide range of experience by doing this.

Radio and TV directors often gain experience by working at small college or community radio or TV stations. Directors can gain experience in many areas of the broadcast industry at these stations.

Directors can gain experience by working at small college or community TV stations.

Chapter 5

The Market

M any people want jobs in the news and entertainment fields. Directors may have a hard time finding jobs because of this. There is a great deal of competition for each job opening.

Earning Jobs

Producers, TV station owners, and radio station owners usually receive many applications for director positions. Applicants must stand out to earn jobs. Applicants must have talent, skills, and knowledge. They must be experienced, hard workers.

Producers and station owners often notice directors who do good work. These producers and station owners may recommend good

Radio directors may start out by working at radio stations.

Producers may notice directors who do good work. This helps the directors find more jobs in the future.

directors to other producers and station owners. This helps directors get other jobs.

Salary

Directors' salaries vary greatly. Directors of major motion pictures may make millions of dollars per year. Directors who cannot find steady work may not earn enough to support themselves. These directors often must take second jobs.

In the United States, most stage directors of small productions earn from $14,000 to $17,000 per year. Stage directors of major productions may earn as much as $80,000 per year. These directors often earn shares of profits as well. This means they earn more money if their productions make large profits.

Directors at small TV and radio stations may earn from $17,000 to $20,000 per year. Experienced directors at major TV and radio stations can earn $100,000 or more.

In Canada, the average salary for creative and performing artists is about $36,000. Directors are in this group. Most directors make between $7,000 and $68,500. But this varies greatly. Successful film directors can earn millions of dollars.

Job Outlook

Inexperienced directors may have difficulty earning enough money to support themselves.

This is because there is a great deal of competition for jobs. But the news and entertainment fields continue to grow around the world. This growth creates new job opportunities.

The TV industry is among the fastest growing entertainment fields in the United States. This is because of the availability of cable TV and satellite systems. Many new TV stations are forming in the United States. This opens up new jobs for directors. But this is not true in Canada. The number of directing jobs in Canada is decreasing.

The future for stage directors is uncertain. Large stage productions have become more popular in recent years. This has led to an increase in jobs for stage directors. But some people fear the U.S. and Canadian governments may soon cut funds for the arts. These funds help support many small stage productions. This could lead to a decrease in stage directing jobs.

Directors may find work in the fast-growing TV industry.

The clapperboard reads:

PROD. NO.
SCENE 1 OBC   TAKE 2   ROLL 56
DATE 10/4   CAM B   SOUND M&O
PROD. NEW WORLD   SYNC
DIRECTOR NICK NICIPHOR
CAMERAMAN GARY GRAVER

Jobs in the radio industry are steady in the United States. These jobs are decreasing in Canada. The radio field offers the best chances for beginning directors to earn jobs. Radio stations in small towns sometimes hire people with little directing experience.

The market for major movies is growing in the United States and Canada. Movie studios are producing more movies every year. This leads to many open jobs. The outlook for film directors is very good.

Advancement

Most directors advance by taking jobs with more responsibilities. For example, co-directors may earn jobs as directors for small productions. They then may earn jobs for larger productions.

Some successful directors become producers. They use their talent, knowledge, and experience to select scripts. They select casts and hire others to direct productions. They may even help new directors begin their careers by giving them jobs.

The job outlook is good for movie directors in the United States and Canada.

Words to Know

amateur (AM-uh-chur)—someone who takes part in an activity for enjoyment rather than money

audition (aw-DISH-uhn)—a tryout for a part in an entertainment or commercial production

budget (BUHJ-it)—a plan for spending money

cast (KAST)—a group of performers who work on a production such as a play, movie, or TV program

rehearsal (ri-HURSS-uhl)—a practice performance

script (SKRIPT)—the written story for a play, movie, TV show, or radio program

storyboard (STOR-ee-bord)—a series of drawings that shows the plot of a TV show or movie

take (TAYK)—an attempt to film a scene for a TV show or movie

To Learn More

Bentley, Nancy and Donna Guthrie. *Putting on a Play: The Young Playwright's Guide to Scripting, Directing, and Performing.* Brookfield, Conn.: Millbrook Press, 1996.

Hahn, Don. *Animation Magic: A Behind-the-Scenes Look at How an Animated Film Is Made.* New York: Disney Press, 1996.

Hayes, Ann. *Onstage & Backstage: At the Night Owl Theater.* San Diego: Harcourt Brace, 1997.

Quinlan, Kathryn A. *Actor.* Careers without College. Mankato, Minn.: Capstone High/Low Books, 1998.

Useful Addresses

American Film Institute (AFI)
Education and Training Programs
2021 North Western Avenue
Los Angeles, CA 90027

Directors Guild of America
7920 Sunset Boulevard
Los Angeles, CA 90046

**International Alliance of Theatrical Stage
Employees, Moving Picture Technicians,
Artists and Allied Crafts of the United States
and Canada (IATSE)—Canadian Office**
258 Adelaide Street East
Suite 403
Toronto, ON M5A 1N1
Canada

Theatre Communications Group
355 Lexington Avenue
New York, NY 10017-0217

Internet Sites

American Federation of Television and Radio Artists
http://www.aftra.com/home.html

Directors Guild of America
http://www.dga.org

Human Resources Development Canada
http://www.hrdc-drhc.gc.ca/JobFutures/english/volume1/513/513.htm

Occupational Outlook Handbook—Actors, Directors, and Producers
http://stats.bls.gov/oco/ocos093.htm

Screen Actors Guild
http://www.sag.com/index2.html

Index